Content Marketing

I0476237

Over 60 Tools to Help you grow your Business and Repurpose your Existing Content

Table Of Contents

Introduction -

I want to thank you and congratulate you for downloading the book, "**Content Marketing: Over 60 Tools to Help you Grow your Business and Repurpose your Existing Content.**"

This book contains proven steps and strategies on how to supercharge your business by repurposing your old content to be able to reach more people and get more customers.

Are you pumping out new content non-stop, but hitting the inevitable roadblock of not being able to keep up? Do you feel as though you are running out of content ideas, and you aren't even sure you are reaching the right people? Repurposing your existing content is the answer to all your worries. It will help you keep your content fresh, and reach new audiences (with a lot less of the work). This book will teach you everything you need to know, which I learned from the best. Consulting with thousands of businesses has taught me the "ins and outs" of content repurposing, and now you too will know how to re-engage your existing audience, as well as how to reach new people.

This book will also guide you through the basics of repurposing: tools you can use, as well as places and strategies to help you use them. This complete package includes the building blocks you need to build a strong foundation. It is sure to help you enhance your content strategy and supercharge your business.

Chapter 1 –

How Can Repurposing Content Supercharge Your Business?

All businesses need to conduct some sort of marketing activity-- be it: paid advertisements, word of mouth, or content. Reaching people is not simple enough. You can end up throwing away a lot of money on ads that don't work. In the early days of content marketing people thought blogging was enough to reach and engage customers, and for a while those companies that were doing it well were crushing it. The internet has changed a lot since then-- we have videos, infographics, apps, podcasts and so much more. So, how do you know what types of content will reach the right people? Creating a variety of different types of content will help you reach different types of people and measure it's results so you know where to focus your efforts. Additionally creating different types of content will re-engage your customers in new ways. Repurposing your content will allow you to keep coming out with fresh content without having to constantly reinvent the wheel, and it will help you avoid problems like these:

- Running out of ideas to write about, make video about, etc.
- Hiring additional writers to come out with fresh content.
- Spending a lot of time creating the content to re-engage the same audience.
- Not reaching different types of customers.
- Being subject to Facebook changes, and Google ranking fluctuations

Individually, these reasons might not seem like much, but when it all stacks up, you can easily feel overwhelmed. That feeling of being overwhelmed will paralyze you and keep your business growth stagnant. Repurposing your existing content will allow you to take a break from having to come up with new and innovative stuff while still staying in front of your audience.

Why should you do it?

a. **It utilizes your posts to their full potential.**

Repurposing your content allows you to stretch the impact of each of your posts, and allows you to use it to its full potential. What do I mean by that? I know you get the idea that coming up with one post involves time and effort. Now it's out there and you have reached some of your target audience and your post served its purpose. What happens next? Repurposing and creating it in different formats will allow you to reach more people on different channels and communicate the same way. It can also spark different ideas on how to add more value to your original posts.

b. **It improves your SEO.**

SEO, or search engine optimization, is something that is either: often overlooked, or it's all some companies focus on. All businesses should be utilizing the amazing resources that the internet provides for marketing and connecting with current and future customers. SEO is key for organic discovery (people finding you through relevant Google searches). Having your SEO dialed in can deliver

1000's of relevant paying customers to your company's website on a daily basis. For those reading who are completely unaware of how SEO works, here's a quick rundown. Google, Bing, and other search engines use tiny bits of computer code to "crawl" your website and identify important keywords on your site, as well as how they rank in comparison to other sites. When someone searches for Sushi in San Francisco they get a variety of responses. SEO will allow you to get on the first page of results and hopefully above the fold (the top half of results you see without having to scroll down). While this book is not about SEO content marketing will help your SEO efforts. When done right you'll start to see traffic increase to your site because of your content. Repurposing will increase the sharing of your content and re-posting on other websites which will increase the links back to your website. Setting up a steady stream of traffic to your site will explode your business and help you grow.

c. **It can attract different types of people.**

Another benefit that you can get from repurposing your content is that you will be able to attract more people and will be able to find new ways to connect with them. You might remember from school that everyone has a different way of learning. There are kinesthetic learners who learn by touch and doing. Then there are visual learners who learn by seeing and reading. Lastly, there are auditory learners, who learn by listening, which is super helpful if you're a college student. When you repurpose, you open your door to all these different kinds of learners.

For example, you started with a blog post or an e-book. Naturally, people who are visual learners will respond best to that post, but what about your auditory and kinesthetic learners? By repurposing your e-book or blog post into a podcast series, audio book, or maybe even a series of instructional videos, you'll be able to reach the other kinds of learners out there. Get the idea, but need help? This book will teach you how to distribute your content to a large quantity of people beyond your current reach.

d. **Widens your reach in different channels.**

Similar to the reasons previously stated repurposing your content will help you reach people across different channels. Not everyone wants to consume content in the same way, some people don't have desktop (or even laptop) computers at home, and don't want to get caught reading personal stuff on their company's time. So are you able to reach them on a mobile device? Additionally not everyone uses Facebook, or perhaps your organic Facebook reach has dropped significantly. By repurposing your content into different mediums you might see an increased reach on your different channels that your customers might have missed at first. So let's say you posted a Top 10 tips to "XXXX" on your social media accounts. As a result you only reached 10 percent of your total followers, and barely received any shares, comments or click-through. Try putting up a quick 30-minute video sharing some tips, and you might see engagement explode. At the time of the writing this book, Facebook is artificially boosting the reach of video content uploaded directly to your Facebook page.

You can also take the video and upload it to Vine, Snapchat, Instagram, YouTube etc. This will result in you impacting a lot more people than you would simply by posting a link to that blog post.

e. **Gets your message reinforced.**

This last benefit of repurposing is easy to understand. Remember when you were little and your Mom repeated certain phrases over and over? Like: "A penny saved is a penny earned," or "Idle hands lead to the devils work," or "If you don't have anything nice to say don't say anything at all." You're parents were reinforcing a message they were trying to communicate to you, and this is something marketing agencies around the world have adopted. It's called the "Rule of Seven." Consumers will need to see your brand and message at least seven times before it starts to take root. Now you can spend a lot of money on ads, and re-target your customers to death. Or you can re-engage them with content, and repurposing your content reinforces your previously delivered messages in a different light.

There are some people who do not believe anything they read easily. Once they read something they just consider it as new information. When they get to see that same message everywhere, and when people start talking about it, then they start to believe it. When a blog post is repurposed into many different formats, the message becomes clearer as it takes on new forms.

Chapter 2 – What Type Of Content Can You Repurpose?

Any content that you have created can be repurposed; even content you haven't created yourself! However knowing what type of content to turn it into can be confusing and for some overwhelming. For the sake of this book I'll start with a blog post and go from there. So let's say you have an epic blog post with the title "10 Secret Ways to Be Productive and Say Goodbye to Procrastination." Here are some different way's your can repurpose that post into different types of content.

- 10 blog posts (1 for each secret way) where you expand upon the ways.

- Presentations: Either the whole post or break down the steps into presentations.

- Videos: Explain the 10 secret steps, or again break it down into a 10 step video series.

- Host a webinar on the topic.

- Create a series of info-graphics relating to the topic.

- Short social media images that will perform well on platforms like Instagram.

- Create an e-book or a real book and upload that to Amazon as a lead magnate and additional stream of revenue.

- Create a 10 steps and e-mail out an auto responder course, where you e-mail your audience a different step each week.

- Create an audio program a podcast or a free audio book.

These are just a few ideas on different ways you could repurpose one simple blog post. Now I don't recommend doing all these things for each and every blog post you've created, as that would become overwhelming and difficult to manage. However as you develop your content marketing strategy you'll find that some of these steps are "must dos" for each piece of content. While on other more epic pieces of content it might make sense to go full force and try to saturate the market with your message.

a. **Blogs**

Blogs started out as online journals, and then evolved into digital magazines and ways for businesses to communicate with their customers outside of traditional advertising and shareholder meetings. Today you'll see thousands of talking heads (myself included) preaching the gospel of blogging and how it can make you rich and famous. While I don't think blogging alone will make you rich or famous it is by far one of the easiest ways to begin content marketing, without needing much money or time to get started.

Now if you already have a blog you'll want to start with your best-performing evergreen content. What is evergreen? Well similar to the trees, evergreen content is content that is consistently popular, and getting read and shared a lot. It's not seasonal, nor does it go viral once, and then drop off. Like the trees it's always growing.

Here's how to determine your evergreen posts:

- Go to Buzzsumo and type in your URL. It will quickly show you the most popular articles based upon social shares. However this is not always the best way to figure it out.
- Use Google analytics to figure out which content has the most readers or incoming links to that article.
- Find Articles with the highest levels of conversions, or engagement. Articles that (if you're able to track) have lead to the most sales, or articles with a lot of comments.

Now social shares are not always the best indicator of success sometimes you can create a great piece of content that is not easily sharable for a variety of reasons. It's not appropriate for most social networks (i.e.: too technical, too niche, or NSFW) For an example I will use a post from Knowledgeformen.com. The author wrote an in-depth article about his issues with porn, masturbation, and his struggle to over come them. If you check out the article it has less than 2,000 social shares. Which makes sense, who wants to share that type of article on Facebook? But after speaking with Andrew the owner of Knowledge for men he gets tens of thousands of visits to his page coming from that article. Psychologists have linked to it, and he's been interviewed many times because of this article.

I share this because it's not always easy to see from the beginning that an article is going to be your most popular. You want to take an analytical approach to figuring that out.

Now if you're just starting a blog or do not have much content from which you can measure, try to make sure that some of the content you're creating is evergreen and not seasonal, and begin your repurposing from there.

b. **Videos**
Videos nowadays are not being used for "entertainment purposes only" anymore. With improvements in camera technology and internet speed you can access videos anywhere and it allows people to create videos about anything. However, making videos for your business does not mean creating traditional style

advertisements. It means creating entertaining and educational content that your audience will love. Now if you've already created video content but found that perhaps the effort is too time consuming and you're limited by your budget or creativity, there are some easy ways to repurpose what you currently have and distribute it to a larger audience.

Some ways of doing this are:

- Typing up transcripts, depending on your budget you can pay a college or high school student to do this. Or you can use a professional service which charges $0.50-$2.00 a minute of audio.

- Chopping up longer video's into shorter segments where you expand on a particular section a little bit more.

- Or you take your shorter videos and combine them into a longer presentation.

- You can combine your videos along similar subjects and create a course on Udemy or other e-learning sites for free, or earn additional revenue.

- Similarly, you can take all that info and turn it into an e-book.

- You can use different services like Wistia to build some interactivity into your videos and collect leads.

- If you're producing some high quality stuff you can capture still images and put some quotes behind it or turn it into a Pinterest infographic.

- Rip the audio from your videos and put them up as Podcast.

Once you have chosen the video, you can create blogs, e-books, infographics and even presentations or podcasts based on it. Just remember to always link it back to the original video or post you're trying to boost. SEO works on YouTube as well or if the videos are hosted on your own site then you'll want that extra SEO "juice" from the backlinks.

c. **Podcasts**

Podcasting is the latest stage in democratization of media, particularly in the audio realm. Before you would have to get on a radio station in order to build an audience, but now anyone can create a podcast and broadcast their ideas and information to the masses. It takes minimal cash to get started and little technical expertise. There are some podcasters making close to $1 million a month from the products and services they offer via their podcast. What makes it powerful from a business prospect is that consumers will typically subscribe to your podcast faster than they would subscribe to your blog or YouTube Channel. So you're able to deliver fresh content right into their ears on a regular basis, without having to worry about a lot about things like e-mail marketing or SEO.

Now if you already have a podcast or if you are planning to start one, you don't have to worry, repurposing podcasts is very similar to your video content.

- You can transcribe the audio into a blog post.

- Create downloadable checklists, or notes from the podcast

- Combine them together to create an audio book, if there are several episodes on a similar topic.

- Create a presentation to go along with the audio book. (I have not found an example of this yet, so I am unsure if this would be an effective use of your time.)

d. **Presentations**

Some people prefer looking at presentations rather than reading blogs, mainly because presentations are colorful and the information is presented in an easily digestible format. Especially for those of us who work in professional services, presentations are a way of life. You can still repurpose these presentations and:

- Turn them into info-graphics.
- Turn them into a series of blog posts.
- Make an e-book where you go into much more detail than you were able to in your slide show.
- Create a video. You can turn your slideshow into a quick video you can speak over for easy-to-make video content.
- Post a podcast. You can turn each slide into it's own episode if the topic can be explored more deeply.

In the resource section of the book I list several places where you can share your presentations so you can expand your reach and audience.

e. **E-books**

E-books are pretty popular these days it seems like every website you go to (including mine) you'll get offered a free e-book in exchange for some personal info (typically an e-mail address). While this is a time proven strategy to build an e-mail list, there's so much more you can be doing. When you visit Amazon, you will see a lot of Kindle books that are easily available to anyone. If you're creating something really valuable you can post it on Amazon and other digital e-book retailers and get them to give it away for free, or you can charge a couple of dollars and create a passive source of income as well as lead generation. There are a lot of best practices for achieving Amazon Kindle success and we won't go over them in depth here, but there are many resources you can find that will teach you better than I can. However some ways you can repurpose an existing book into the following:

- You can create snippets of your book and get them published on blogs, newspapers, and magazines other than yours. This was a technique used by the creators of *Chicken Soup for the Soul*. They published snippets of the stories in the book with a little note at the end telling them to check out the full story in their book.
- You can turn the subject into a smaller video series or course. This is typically done in the reverse though. People will create courses that cost hundreds of dollars and then publish a book in order to get you to purchase the course or attend a live training.

Depending on the subject you can create a graphic novel. I've seen this done a few times with business and I've seen the US Army do this with things like safety manuals. It turns a subject like "learning the maximum load of some piece of equipment" into a slightly more entertaining format.

Chapter 3 – Turn Them Into Different Formats

Sometimes figuring out what format to turn your existing content too can be confusing or overwhelming. Will your blog be better if you repurpose it into a video or a presentation? Or would your video be better if you create a slideshow for it or an infographic? These questions sometimes stop business owners from even starting with a content marketing effort.

Whether you can relate to the questions above or not, I'm here to tell you that there are no right or wrong answers in repurposing. Any content can be turned into a different format. You just have to know your strengths and weaknesses and what types of content your customers want. If you are a strong writer then by all means stick with blogging. If you're good at public speaking or speaking in general then create videos, don't worry about the editing part you can find someone on Elance to edit them for $10. If you're a visual person with an eye for design then create compelling graphics. If you're still lost here are some basic idea's to get you started.

1. Figure out your ideal customer and how they spend their day, consume content, and look for purchasing information. This isn't as hard as it sounds. You can look at what a successful competitor is doing in the space and replicate their efforts.

2. Once you've determined what channels of distribution you're going to use (YouTube, Blogging, Pinterest, Facebook, Instragam, LinkedIn, and so on) figure out the best practices for each of those channels. These best practices will change every six months to a year, so be sure to keep your search to more recent information.

3. Set your purpose and experiment. Figure out what the goal is of your repurposing efforts, and make sure it's something easily quantifiable or measurable. So if you're goal is to increase opt-ins to your e-mail list then you want to try your repurposing efforts for a bit and see if there is any increase in opt-ins and if you can attribute that directly to your content efforts as opposed

to something else. If after a set period of time (I would recommend 30-60 days) it's not working, then move on and try something else.

Tweak and modify your approach to amplify the results. When you first start out you may see some results but maybe it's not on the level you were hoping for. Now this can sometimes be attributed to other factors beyond your content. Take the e-mail opt in example. Is your website following the best practices for e-mail opt-in conversions? Does your repurposed content have a strong call to action and branding? A lot of people when they start out forget these basics and with a few tweaks and optimizations they can start seeing explosive growth.

Chapter 4 – Add New Materials

One good way to repurpose your content to supercharge your business is to add new material to old posts. This way you can turn your past successes into repeat successes by freshening up old materials.

Refresh your old posts with new information.

Old posts tend to get forgotten. The only way that these posts will still be visited is when you promote them every now and then. Unless they are so epic in nature that people continue to link to them and share them. On the other hand, if you keep promoting the same content over and over again, you'll see diminishing returns. Adding new information to old posts is the recycling of the content world.

- Has something in the industry changed, things that were once thought to be true, no longer are? Maybe you did an article on how to engage your fans on Facebook but recent changes to Facebook made that information not so relevant?

Update it and re-engage all those past readers.

- Did you have a success with something you tried and posted about? Then tell that success story. Or if you failed tell that story as well.

- Did a customer write you and tell you how your advice or tips caused them to succeed. Customer testimonials like that are a powerful piece of content that can drive sales and business growth.

- Perhaps you wrote a decent sized post that got good engagement that you could expand into an EPIC post.

In adding new information, you can add anything, just remember to consider who your target audience is, and what will keep them hooked. This makes things like guest posting and re-posting on other platforms easier without having to create something entirely new. You can reference and old post and drive traffic back to that post.

Chapter 5 – Turn Your Top 10 into 10 Posts Or Vice Versa

Whether you are planning to repurpose for a blog or a video, the ultimate objective is to market content effectively in order to relay information and attract the attention of viewers. In order to effectively do this it implies that summarizing and organizing information into a list is an effective marketing method to increase the interest and the volume of viewers. Such method involves ranking content parts in a hierarchy in order to gather the most important information. Think about how many 10 reasons for XYZ posts you see on Facebook, Twitter, Pinterest and other channels. There is a reason for that, it's because they work. Perhaps this is old news for you and you've already been producing top 10 posts; below are some strategies on how to take those existing posts and expand.

a. **Create individual posts for every item.**

So you already have several Top 10 posts (the number doesn't need to be limited to 10 it can be more or less) you can take each bullet point and expand it. If you're a decent content creator you've already posted some information. Hopefully your top lists don't look like this.

Top Ways to Overcome Writer's Block

1. Try "free association."

2. Get out and exercise.

3. Meditate.

4. Look at what someone else has done and start expanding on that idea.

5. Try talking about a subject and record your thoughts for later transcription.

While the information provided is useful it lacks substance. Maybe the reader doesn't know what free association is or thinks meditation is a weird thing only Buddhists do. Hopefully you added a short paragraph supporting each one of your points. Now you can take that paragraph and write a longer post on free association, what it is, how to do it, and famous authors who have already done it. You could even write a small book on the benefits of mediation, how to do it, or even talk about the myths and misconceptions people have about it. If you do this for some of your most popular list-posts you should see explosive engagements.

b. **Create a top 3, 5 or 10 for several posts.**

This is taking the same concept as previously mentioned and reversing it. If you take several expansive posts around a similar theme or even a theme that you can loosely associate you can create a Top 10 article. Done right, these lists will become high impact summaries of the content you've already created. It also engages users who have a shorter attention span. As maybe they don't have time to read your epic post about whatever or watch that 30 minute YouTube video, they just want the highlights. They want to get the juicy bits and get on with their day. The Top 10 post accomplishes that in an easy to read manner.

c. **Curate posts that have the same topic as you.**

Curating content on its surface may not seem like a repurposing strategy. However there is no rule that says you must repurpose your own content. You can take content that other people have created, and turn into something else. This provides many different opportunities to connect with other thought leaders or businesses in your industry. The guy who runs video fruit, Bryan Harris, gained traction by going to popular bloggers and turning some of their most popular posts into videos for them free of charge. This strategy worked well for him as he was trying to grow his video production company and did not have an audience of his own. So by repurposing other peoples content into something valuable for his own audience as well as the influencers he was able to get shout outs, endorsements, and links back to his own blog (important for SEO).

Now maybe you're thinking, "That is great for him, but I don't have time or the skills to be making these videos." That's fine, you can still use this in effective manner that you can outsource if you lack time or do yourself if you have time and no money. This is particularly helpful if you're starting your content marketing strategy and haven't had time to develop your strategy yet. Here are some basic steps you can take to help you curate other people's content.

1. First decide what topics you're going to curate for. Then you can do a Google search for those topics to see what you find. I have a list of several tools you can use to help with this in my book, *More than 60 Ultra Hot Resources to Help you Develop Kick-Butt Ideas for your Blog*.

2. Start collecting links and summarizing the key points in the content in whatever medium you're using. It doesn't have to be the same as the content you're curating. For example you could record your thoughts on four to five articles you read that morning on the importance of sleep for overall

health, and post that on YouTube (if you're covering a health related topic). Or you could summarize two to three videos in a blog post so people who don't have time to watch three 20-minute videos can get the key points from you.

3. Share what you've done with those influencers and content creators. You'll be surprised what happens, you might get a re-tweet, a share, a blog mention, or more. If you're really good at SEO and that article is highly searched, shared, or indexed, your response to that might just get ranked slightly below it, or if you're really lucky right above it.

4. Look at the comments in the other content creators post and see what type of questions and themes stand out, collect those ideas and turn them into a post expanding upon ideas that the original thought leader didn't have time to explain or perhaps couldn't due to a lack of knowledge.

This is not limited to summaries and expressing your thoughts on a subject if you're an artistic individual you can create visual representations of data presented in an article, video, speech etc. A great deal of information in this book was notes I collected from reading hundreds of blog articles and videos that I've combined with my own first-hand knowledge.

Chapter 6 – Grow Your Posts into Something Epic

So let's say you've written one really good post, have a really popular video, or a podcast episode that is highly downloaded. In that piece of content you might have introduced other concepts and topics that you were not able to fully explore at the time for a variety of reasons. Well now is the time to expand on those subtopics and ideas into something epic! Here are some steps to help get you started.

a. **Pick your post and outline the subjects and topics you wish to expand on.**

   This is the starting of your content creation process but doesn't have to be the first part of your new epic post or series of posts. It might be necessary to provide more back-story or a different structure to your new epic post. However for the sake of your SEO efforts **DO NOT** take down that post as it might mess up your ranking and back links. If you want to create a new bigger post, or series of posts, summarize that one and link back to for those that want to more info.

b. **Start expanding on those subjects and topics.**

This is where the content creation begins, but you do not have to do all the work yourself you can use the content creation methods I mentioned in the previous chapter to help get you going. While you're creating these expanded topics think about other pieces of content that this is similar to.

Depending on how you're doing this you might want to keep a consistent theme throughout your posts so they flow and are more coherent. Though you could also create your own glossary or resource page where you're defining and explaining terms and concepts in your industry in-depth. If you're a mechanic, you could create a plethora of content explaining what each part of the engine does, why it breaks down, and how much it might cost to replace. If you're a doctor, you might want to explain a bunch of medical terms to people, or basic ailments that are easily avoidable and how to avoid them. If you write about internet marketing you might create a guide about all the terms internet marketers throw around like, SEO, back links, black hats, white hats, CPC, CTR and so on. As you do this you might find other topics and ideas to expand on, but you want to stick with your original outline first before going to other topics so you don't get sucked down a rabbit hole and never finish anything.

c. **Connect everything.**

Once you're finished creating your content start linking it to other articles, videos, and podcasts on your blog, or content channel. This is what is known as on-site SEO. It helps your site or content channel in ways I don't want to get into in this book but it helps your ranking and helps get your audience more engaged, as the additional information will be easier to find and connect with. You can also take that new piece of content that you've created and start sharing it with other content creators. As mentioned previously this strategy, when done right, will lead to valuable links back to your site, which is important to your SEO efforts.

d. **Turn blogs into videos.**

Let's say you have a blog, and you want to venture into YouTube or Vimeo to be able to reach more people. Here are some tips:

Slideshow Video. Let's say your blog post has a lot of photos, you can compile all of them and make a slideshow video. There is a lot of different software out there that can create your videos for you. You just have to do certain edits, like the time that the photos will appear, their transition, the background music and some texts. You can even find someone on Fiverr.com or Elance.com to do this for you for around $40-50.

Regular Videos and "Vlogs." Let's say you are not camera shy, you can invest in a good camera and create a video of you or yourself doing what you are blogging about. You really don't even need to buy a nice camera your cellphone and laptop cameras are sufficient if you're just starting out. These are particularly effective if you're trying to sell something specific in the video because you're enthusiasm will come through and seeing your face will allow customers to connect with you.

Text Video/ Infographic Videos. These are videos with animated text or basic animation of an existing info-graphic that you already have. These are particularly effective for conveying quick ideas and concepts. You can do this if you are camera shy and putting your face out there to the masses terrifies you. Again if you're lacking the technical skill you can outsource these videos cost effectively, and you can even have someone narrate it for you. A 30 second video might cost you between $50-100. If you're strapped for cash, or a do-it yourselfer there are some sites and tools that will help you get this done in the resource section of this book.

Chapter 7 – Basics Of Repurposing

a. **Create**

Now that you've learned some basics it's time to create. What you have to do is to browse on your content and see if there are things worth repurposing. You already know that you can repurpose any content. If you have seen an article that performs better than others, pick it up and start with that one right away.

If you're still unsure about what you should do, just start creating different types of content until you find something that clicks with you. You never know what's going to work best for you unless you already have some experience or expertise. Even if you're doing something similar to a competitor because you think it might be working for them, you might find out that they're wrong. So if you're lost start with some of these basic repurposing formats.

Slideshow. When you're making a slide show, make sure that the presentation can be read well and is pleasing to the eyes. Avoid having too much color and animation. The important thing is to present the text clearly and the points should be well delivered to the viewer. It's also better if you present some slides with photos or images for each point tackled. If you really feel like your presentation is no good, then outsource it someone on Fiverr. For $5-20 bucks you can get some pretty impressive design work done.

Webinar. Webinars are particularly effective for businesses that are trying to sell something. However you don't always need to be selling, and while this sounds expensive you can do this cheaply with Google Hangouts and some WordPress templates. You can then record the webinar and post it on your YouTube Channel.

Video. Start off recording some simple videos explaining the content of your article or other piece of content. Or some how-to videos can be done quickly and easily from your cellphone. My advice is to do three takes of the video if possible as you might mess up at first, but instead of pausing just keep going. Next time you record it will be a little better, and by the third time it will feel more natural. If you are going to be using your cellphone, I would recommend investing $10-20 on a little phone tripod for a slightly smoother shot, and getting a memory card for your phone. If you have the budget you can have people create videos for you. Similar to what the Video Fruit guys have done, or you can go to Fiverr and find someone to make you a decent video for less than $50.

Infographics: You don't need expensive design software or even an amazing set of design skills. You can use free tools likes Canva and the other tools I list in the resource section of the book, or again you can have them outsourced.

b. **Reach Out**

In the resource section of the book, we not only have links to tools to help you create new content but also places you can distribute it. While that is a great place to start it's only the beginning and you should expand your efforts beyond the tools and places listed in this book. Here are some strategies to help you gain more exposure and distribution for your newly repurposed content.

c. **Promote via social media.**

This one is pretty basic, your business should have all it's social media bases covered. Facebook, Twitter, and Linkedin at the minimum. You should do a bit of analysis to see if Pinterest, Instagram, Vine, or other social channels will work for your business and content type. I would recommend testing a bit, because you never know-- something that you might think will never work on Pinterest might just become your best source of leads. Sometimes it's not about quantity but the quality of the traffic. Almost all of these platforms have paid methods to boost the reach of your content. While this book doesn't cover that, a simple Google search can teach you some best practices and tips to get the types of results you want.

d. **Build an E-mail list**

If you don't already have an e-mail list, start building one. The problem a lot of smaller businesses run into is that they build their entire marketing efforts on one platform like Facebook, and then when Facebook decides to reduce the reach of fan pages so that you have to "pay to play," you're screwed. Building an e-mail list is a great way to reconnect with your customers over and over again. It ensures that you can almost always reach them.

e. **Reach out to influencers and other companies.**

There are a lot of media properties that are constantly looking for writers who are interested in posting original content to their platform. Reach out to some that might reach your target audience. If you're not sure, try to find a copy of their media kit and that will almost always have stats and demographic data of their audience. This could turn into a very powerful distribution channel for you if you can get on a couple of bigger properties. It doesn't even need to be digital you can find magazines and newspapers that are always looking for content to fill their pages for cheap. You can also reach out to influencers in your industry and share with them your content and ideas.

f. **Pay for Distribution**

There are more and more content distribution platforms popping up out there, from Mylikes, to Outbrain, Taboola,

Yahoo! and now even StumbleUpon. If you have the budget (Typically as little as $20 a day) you can pay to have your content distributed across the web. The best part is that this is all on a performance basis, so if someone doesn't visit your page you don't pay.

Chapter 8 – Common Content Marketing Myths To Avoid

Here are some common myths that you may want to stay clear off:

a. **Longer is always better.**

It is true that longer articles that are more in depth tend to get more shares, link backs, and so on. But this is not true for every business or industry. It really comes down to your goals with your content. While we all strive to create something interesting and valuable to our audience there will be times when you just don't have the time or energy to write an epic 5,000 word post full of detailed research-- you have a business to run.

Here are some tips to make it as short and crisp as possible:

- Headlines matter, you want your headline to draw them in without giving it all away. When you start out try creating 10-20 headline variations.

- Use sub-headers. When looking at a post, readers tend to look for the sub headers or the bulleted list first. When they don't find one, they might not continue reading.

- Make sure it loads well on a mobile device and is easy to read. Your content may look great on your laptop, but does it load the same way on a tablet or phone?

b. **More posts= more reach.**

Having more posts does not always mean you'll reach more people. Sometimes it just means that you have too much to manage. You need to decide on the frequency of your content creation process and repurposing. Perhaps you don't have time to create something awesome every day or even every week that is fine. Create one awesome piece of content a month. Then use the repurposing techniques described in this book to get that post more exposure and engagement with your audience without constantly having to be super creative.

c. **Content marketing can be passive**

Contrary to what other people believe, content marketing is not passive. Especially in the beginning, while you are gathering up your audience, you cannot expect content marketing to be passive. It takes a lot of work to build up an audience especially if you're starting from scratch. So gather up your resources and prepare a game plan. Your business is not going anywhere unless you take it there.

Remember to take one step at a time. If you want to try all the different types of formats, don't do everything at once. Concentrate on one format first. Take note of the key points: create, reach out, promote. Be sure to have clear goals for your content so that you can measure the results effectively and see if you're efforts are producing your desired results. It's going to take time and effort. Trust me, I have a full time position where I'm building a sales team from the ground up, in addition to building my many side businesses. Content marketing takes time and deliberate effort, but if you stick with it and work on small improvement you'll see your business start to grow.

Resources for Repurposing your Content -

Syndication-- looking for an easy way to repurpose your old content? Syndication is the best way to do this, and it is also a sure-fire way to continue benefiting from your past work. Not sure what syndication is? It is the act of reposting your existing content, the way that it is, on other websites. You may be wondering how this could possibly hurt your SEO efforts, and whether someone with a higher page rank and greater domain authority might rank higher with your content. There is a pretty good chance that someone will outrank you, if they have a higher authority, but don't let this stop you. Part of their ranking will actually be passed down to you. Here are some guidelines to consider when you are syndicating your previous posts:

1. Canonical tags: If a site is going to repurpose your content on their own site without making any changes, it is wise to ask them to implement a "rel=canonical" tag to the page your original article is on. This will allow

any page rank the other site gets to
be passed on to you.

2. No index Meta Tags: Similar to
number one, this is a great tip when
you are allowing a website to post
your content without enough
changes to be considered different.
Have the other site implement this
tag. This will tell Google not to index
the page. <meta name="robots"
content="noindex">

3. Link to your site: Let's say the other
site won't do any of these things
because either they can't, or want
the page rank for themselves. That
means you get them a regular text
link to where the original content is
hosted. Google is pretty smart at
figuring this stuff out so they'll see
that you created the content first.

#1 – Medium

Medium is a popular publishing platform because it's easy to use, the content you publish looks great on any device, and it can help expand your audience. Anyone can create an account on Medium and publish a story. The platform will share your content with others based on engagement and other factors. This is a good option for people who have a small audience on a different platform and want to quickly share some repurposed content in order to expand their current audience.

Quick Tip: You should always try to take a new approach to republished blog content. It doesn't have to be an exact replica-- and in fact, it probably shouldn't be. Try writing a new headline, or add/remove content from the original version of the article to create a more original post. Sites like Medium do best when sharing personal stories, so try adding a personal touch! It is always a nice way to change things up.

#2 – Social Media Today

Social Media Today is a syndication site that allows users to submit stories manually through an RSS feed. Keep in mind, just because something has been submitted on this site does not mean it is going to be published. The editors of SMT review the content and select the best stories to feature on their homepage. Do you have an RSS feed set up on your site, and think you have something to say about the topics covered by Social Media Today? It's probably time to get submitting! This is a great platform for older content that originally got a lot of engagement with your audience, but has since lost traction.

#3 – Growth Hackers

GrowthHackers.com is a community of marketing and "growth hacking" professionals who submit related topics, which are then ranked similar to Reddit's upvoting system. If you have an interesting story or case study about how you went from A to Z, this is the place to share it. There are also a lot of great tips on how to grow your own business.

Remember the key to any community like this is not just posting your own links or relevant content, but also engaging with that community. Do yourself a favor and spend a few days engaging with particular posts you like before posting anything of your own.

#4 – Inbound

This site is pretty similar to GrowthHackers but its guidelines are a little stricter. It is important to pay attention to their rules, and make sure that your content is relevant to the audience.

#5 – Biz Sugar

BizSugar is another content-syndication site, but with a broader focus of small businesses. Publishers on this site focus on topics that business owners can relate to, such as management techniques, accounting problems, marketing, sales, etc.

#6 – Reddit

Reddit describes itself as the front page of the internet, and rightly so. Almost everything that goes viral online first started on Reddit. Someone I know once described Reddit as a place you can go to get "super geeky" about any topic that you are passionate about. This could be anything from new technology, to the latest Sherlock Holmes fan fiction, and so much more. There are thousands of "subreddits" that are grouped by topic. For many content creators, Reddit is a huge source of traffic and can drive thousands of clicks. However, before you go and start posting away, be sure to read each subreddit's submission guidelines and start off by engaging with already popular or new posts, before you share. Reddit is a self-policing community, with some additional technology built in to help prevent people from gaming the system.

#8 – Examiner

Examiner is a curated community news source. Its articles are written by thousands of independent writers from around the world and they cover a very wide array of subjects. Unlike other sites like Medium, you do need to first apply and be approved to submit articles. <u>You can apply here.</u>

#9 – Business 2 Community

This is like Examiner, but focused more on business topics. They allow writers to submit and syndicate content, but their guidelines are pretty strict. You can see the <u>guidelines here</u>. This is a great place to publish your repurposed content because B2C get's syndicated on sites like *Yahoo News* so the potential for greater exposure is huge.

Extend your Reach with these Underutilized Social Media Sites -

We all know everyone and their mom knows how to use Facebook, Twitter, Pinterest, and Instagram, but the truth is, there are so many other great social media platforms out there. Check out these sites as a starting place to expand your reach. Keep in mind, the key to success on any social network is interacting with the community, and providing valuable content for its members.

#11 – Quora

Quora is one of the better "question and answer" sites on the web. You can easily find people who are looking for the answers you have. You can follow different subjects and different people. This can be a great research tool as well, since you can ask questions and get some decent answers from knowledgeable people. You can also upload content directly to your profile, or share snippets of your content that you choose.

#12 – Become A LinkedIn Publisher

LinkedIn is a very valuable resume tool and professional resource, but did you also know that it serves as an equally great publishing platform? All LinkedIn users are able to publish any kind of content on their profile that they choose. Doing this, along with some LinkedIn profile optimization (INSERT PROFILE OPTIMIZATION TOOL) can really amp up your reach if you're in a B2B Space or on looking for a new gig. It allows you to show off your content as well as the social proof of your resume. Here are some tips for optimizing your LinkedIn content efforts.

LinkedIn is a great place for repurposing your content, because you can share your work with all different kinds of relevant groups. Want to take your LinkedIn game to the next level? Try creating a group and organizing conversations around your areas or expertise. Lewis Howes credits this technique to his success, and has even put together a course on the subject that you can check out here.

#13 – Google+ (Long-Format)

Google+ is often ignored by most people, but actually has a very active core group of users. Google+ allows you share up to 10,000 characters of content, which makes it ideal for long format, highly visual work. In addition to sharing various types of content (photos, blog posts, short videos), you can also use Google Hangouts to record sessions with your audience or industry experts. Think about how cool it would be to host an interactive session with an industry expert where your audience could participate and ask questions live! You're also able to record the session then share them with your followers elsewhere.

#14 – StumbleUpon Paid and Free Campaigns.

StumbleUpon has lost a lot of the limelight it had a few years ago, however it's still a great place to get your content out there and in front of new users. You have two basic options: a paid membership, or free one. While free is always good you might want to consider the paid membership as well. The good thing about their paid option is that it's a self-service platform so you can submit your links and set a daily budget and CPC. If your content is engaging, StumbleUpon will boost discovery in its organic "stumbles." You can test out which content will work best by having a few friends or freelancers submit your content to StumbleUpon for you, and then you can check your analytics to gauge which article got the most traffic. You can set your desired budget daily and traffic is delivered on a cost per click basis.

StumbleUpon, much like many other available traffic sources on the web, has the potential to be a very valuable resource. If used correctly it is a great way to attract more followers, build links, and even grow your brand awareness. However, placed in the wrong hands and it will only result in tiring efforts and high bounce rates.

It has been said (by Ross Hudgens of Siege Media) that StumbleUpon can "essentially serve as a thousand dodge balls being thrown at a wall. Visitors, like dodge balls, quickly bounce, and without another person to return the throw, they are extremely unlikely to return." At first, StumbleUpon appears to drive large amounts of traffic to your site, but then you may realize that the traffic isn't actually doing much for you in the grand scheme of things. Many people decide to give up on the service as soon as they realize this unfortunate fact.

The key to adequately increasing traffic with StumbleUpon is to know how to balance conversion rates and traffic volumes, in order to gain a greater net benefit. You will need to gain a better understanding of how to target the right demographics and create successful StumbleUpon content, as well as know what to do with the visitors when they come, in order to take advantage of the increase in traffic.

Hop off the rollercoaster of emotions that StumbleUpon may have already offered you a ride on. Keep reading this article in order to discover new ways to use StumbleUpon. Let's start with the basics. First we will take a look at how to increase traffic via StumbleUpon in the first place.

Understanding StumbleUpon Advertising:

StumbleUpon gives users the opportunity to practice inbound marketing through advertising. I know what you're thinking—how does this even make sense? Advertising is usually known as a form of outbound marketing... if you are trying to sell a product to a customer. The thing with content marketing is, if done right, you should hopefully be able to generate visitors at hardly any cost. The key to successful content marketing begins with the content itself. With StumbleUpon advertising, all you have to do is put forth the effort to provide strong, authentic content, and ideally, multitudes of visitors will follow.

In the past, you would have had to rely on the standard methods of StumbleUpon— creating a profile and submitting your content into the swimming pool of pages waiting to be stumbled on, hoping that it will pick up momentum with the first few people who happen to come across it. Now, with StumbleUpon campaigns, your content becomes the ad people will see when they are stumbling. Ideally, it should cost you under $20, and take less than 24 hours for you to determine whether your content will be successful. In the past, there really wasn't a sure-fire way to know whether your efforts were working. Wouldn't you rather have a definitive idea of what works, and what doesn't? Now you can quit wasting your precious time, and discover the answers you need as you go.

The Research Behind the Content:

Let's delve deeper into the topic of content marketing. As mentioned above, successful content will drive visitors to your site via StumbleUpon campaigns, but there is more to it than just that. Rather than focusing on fashioning creative authentic content that you "think" will work, it is important to actually put some research into your efforts. As a strong content marketer, it is best to start your content building process by researching demographics from StumbleUpon's interest groups. You will want to create your content based on the results of your research.

The neat thing about StumbleUpon is that you have the ability to reach your target markets individually, as well as to utilize the service's own unique interest groups to create successful content, that might not pick up any momentum elsewhere. The following is a list of variables you might want to consider when you are trying to plan which demographics to target: location, browser type, interest, age range, and gender of the individuals you are expecting your content to appeal to.

Creating Successful Content on StumbleUpon:

When it comes to successful content creation, a strong rule of thumb to follow is this: simplicity is best. You want your content to be easy to read and process. Keep in mind that most people who come across your content may not stop to read the whole thing in its entirety. It is best if they are able to comprehend the "just" of it, simply by scanning through the page. You can achieve this by including bold print, images, and info graphics into the content. The more text-heavy, and complex your content is, the higher your site bounce rate will be. This is especially true when it comes to StumbleUpon.

The very nature of StumbleUpon is being able to easily come across content. Individuals who use the service don't want to have to work to gain knowledge, or be entertained. They use StumbleUpon to simply be able to do just that... stumble upon creative content that catches their eye, and will quickly result in some form of benefit to them.

Hudgens, mentioned above (from Siege Media), recommends that content marketers who are looking to successfully build a following from StumbleUpon should "build content that would still be interesting if all normally formatted copy was removed." Images, and easy-to-read text is key to successful stumbling. Copy-heavy content should be avoided at all costs.

In his own *Advanced Guide to StumbleUpon Marketing*, Hudgens offers these examples of successful content:

17 Practical Uses for Lego in Your Everyday Life on Mashable

9 Reasons You Should Eat Cabbage on EcoWatch

The Top 75 Pictures of the Year for 2013 on artFido

What Pets Want, a curation project

What if the NFL Logos Were Hipsters? On Kissing Suzy Kolber

A great way to get an idea of what works (*and what doesn't*) on StumbleUpon is to become the consumer. Create a profile and start stumbling! You will quickly be able to point out what you think is successful content, and then create some of your own.

Why $20 is all you Need:

Ross Hudgens introduced to his viewers something called the "$20 Paid Discovery Promotion Formula." He has tried and tested the idea that all you need to do is set up your paid advertising campaigns on StumbleUpon with the following structure: **a budget of $10 a day, over the course of two days, with your maximum spend set to $20**. He thinks the "price per stumble" point should land somewhere between twelve and sixteen cents only.

This formula should benefit you in the following ways:

· It will give you a significant enough sample size to decide whether your content is right for StumbleUpon.

· It will help you monitor your content over the time period of two days, in order to help you discern whether your content will be successful.

A good way to determine whether your content is performing adequately is to gauge how many earned visitors you are receiving. You will also want to pay attention to the information found on your StumbleUpon dashboard, such as how many likes you are getting per page views. Hudgens says he is satisfied when he sees a 10% ratio of likes to views, but it should be noted that each industry is unique. You will want to re-evaluate your spending if you notice that after two days you have fewer than 100 page views, and no likes.

Building your StumbleUpon Audience:

As mentioned before, building your audience begins by first researching ideal target demographics, and then creating authentic content that will appeal to them and what they are looking for.

You will only be able to attract the attention of long-term followers if you regularly provide them with easy-to-find, and easy-to-read content. Once you have found a demographic and successfully marketed your content to them, you will want to keep at it. Continue to place content they are interested right in front of their eyes, and they *should* continue to click on it. Once you get them coming back to your site enough times they will be hooked, and become a returning visitor. If you only target certain groups in varied bursts, you will continue to have a high bounce rate and little ROI.

Viral content is possible on StumbleUpon, and may be great for your demographics temporarily, but this is not something that should be relied on. Strategy and consistency will win the race.

How to Hook your Readers:

The strategies that you will use to hook your readers on StumbleUpon are really no different that those you would use anywhere else on the web—but still important nonetheless. Here are some great strategies that have been proven successful when it comes to grabbing the attention of your viewers (keep in mind that these are just a few of many):

· Incorporating social media, such as Facebook and Google+ like boxes and hooks, midway through the page.

· Setting up a Tweet button on your page, to engage viewers on that platform.

· Using email signups to get your readers contact information, in order to follow up with them later on.

· Retargeting visitors, and getting the back to your site after the first initial visit.

· Including a value-based offer, or compelling call to action at the end of your content.

· Optimizing your site's landing page.

· Using pop up windows to collect information, such as emails.

· Creating STRONG content.

Additional Tips to help you Increase your ROI:

Here are a few additional tips and tactics that might help you get closer to achieving a positive ROI.

· Keep in mind that mostly women use StumbleUpon, and female-focused content tends to perform better. There is a good chance that you will get a positive influx of female visitors when you use female-focused images in your StumbleUpon content.

· Be careful not to over segment your audience. The market on StumbleUpon isn't as large as it is elsewhere on the web, and if you over segment, you will most likely take a hit to the number of visitors you have coming to your content. As Hudgens says, "The more you dice up your content, the smaller your audience can become—which means it might go 'hot' only and only get you about 1000 total visits."

· Use StumbleUpon as a stepping-stone, for determining where you will take your content in the future. StumbleUpon is a great way to figure out if your content will be successful, and if you should pursue other similar content on your site. It is also important for you to keep in mind that StumbleUpon is a unique traffic source, and even if your content isn't immediately successful on StumbleUpon, you still may be able to find success with it elsewhere.

· Consider adding social buttons to your content. Social validation is a great way to get people interested in your content before they have even taken the first initial look. People trust the opinions of fellow consumers more than they trust the marketers

Repurpose your Content as an Online Resource -

If you've created enough content around one subject you might want to consider turning it into an online course. Not only will this enhance your status as an expert in your industry it can also be a decent source of passive income. Creating a course is a more active way to repurpose your content, and it almost always guarantees dividends in the future.

#16 – Udemy

Udemy is one of the leading marketplaces for online courses. The site offers curriculum on basically anything you can think of, varying from how to code HTML to how to do a juice cleanse, and so much more. Udemy is free to use, and the format is pretty simple. You can utilize tools such as Camtasia and Screenflow to record your class on your own computer screen, or you can rent a camera to record yourself as you discuss and demonstrate the topics that you would like to present. You can also break topics down into modules, and expand on them by offering homework and quizzes. You can either give your course away for free, or charge money for it if you think people will buy it. One highly recommended strategy is to start by giving away your course for free, and then begin charging for it after you've refined it a couple of times and gotten enough people interested in it. Udemy only has a couple of rules: the content you upload has to be mostly original, and a large portion of it needs to be exclusive to the site. This works great for people who are expanding on their pre-existing content, but if you think you're just going to be able take some old YouTube videos that you made a while back and throw them up as a course, you will need to either first remove the videos from YouTube, or rethink your strategy.

#17 – Skillshare

SkillShare is similar to Udemy, as it is a community of teachers and students. The site offers a wide variety of courses covering every subject you can think up. What makes them different from Udemy is that they created a membership-operated site. Instead of purchasing individual courses (like on Udemy), customers pay for a membership and have access to all the courses on the site. Users can also access your courses for free but will have to tolerate ads coming up on the site. If you're interested in earning money, Udemy is probably the better option. The payments for SkillShare work similar to Amazon's "Unlimited" program. They go a little something like this:

#18 – Guides.co

Guides.co is less of place to share content, and more of a content-creation platform that you can use to make interactive guides for your audience. It may not help you reach a new audience, but it can help increase your audience engagement and make your content look great. It has an easy to use interface that is very visually appealing. You are able to upload your work for people to discover, but I wouldn't count on it as a source of large amounts of new traffic.

#19 – Helpouts by Google

Helpouts is Google's version of Clarity.fm, which allows you to offer live video help based on your expertise. You can charge for this help or give it away for free. Both Helpouts and Clarity are great, though Helpouts seems to cover a broader range of topics. It might be a better fit than clarity if you are trying to reach a more consumer-focused audience. Maybe you run a cooking blog and want to help people make your signature dish, or maybe you're a fitness expert and you want to help people lose weight. Helpouts is the perfect forum for you to find and help people in your ideal area of reach.

#20 Clarity.FM

Similar to Helpouts, but focused more on business topics and less on consumer issues. All the coaching or advice you give is done over the phone. You can see an example of my profile here.
https://clarity.fm/jeremiahboehner

While mine is a little lackluster, here are some examples of accounts from people who are earning a lot from this channel.

https://clarity.fm/amyporterfield

https://clarity.fm/lewishowes

https://clarity.fm/adii

They've also built a Quora like platform where you can answer questions for free which can help you build credibility if you don't already have a decent following. This platform is great if you're target audience is mostly business professional of some sort.

Create a Slide Deck to Repurpose your Content -

Making slideshows out of your existing content is an excellent way to further communicate the same ideas on several different platforms. Not much of a designer? Does the idea of putting together slideshows sound terrifying and time-consuming? Good news-- there are a couple of great resources that you can use to quickly and easily put some together, or find someone else to do it for you.

1. Fiverr- There are a lot of great slideshow-designers on Fiverr, but unfortunately, in order to find them you usually have to weed out a lot of crappy ones. You can find one person that I have used in the past and would recommend <u>here</u>. You can find examples of her work <u>here</u> and <u>here</u>.
2. Odesk, Elance, and other, freelance/contracting sites: On these sites, you can easily find freelancers to help you transform your work into slideshows for relatively cheap.

3. Canva.com: Canva.com is a new, online editing tool that has been making some large waves recently. It's a content-creating tool that makes it fast and easy to create some great looking projects ranging from one sheets, to social media posts, and of course slideshows. The best part it is, it's free to use. They do have some paid upgrades for better graphics and features, but the free version is quick and easy to use.

4. Prezi: Prezi is another great online presentation software. It differs from PowerPoint, Canva, and Google Docs by helping people to create really unique and dynamic looking presentations. It is especially popular with college kids, and sales teams looking to make a great impact on their customers. The software also doubles as a collaboration tool, so you can have your entire teamwork on one project simultaneously.

There are a lot of different places for you to share your work once you have created your content into slideshows. Here are a few:

#20 – Slideshare

Slideshare is the largest community for uploading your presentations. You can upload and share your work in both PDF or PowerPoint formats. This is a great way to grow your audience and share interesting content with your followers. In addition to the site's sharing features, it also helps you build codes to easily embed your slideshows on your site, as well as other sites.

#21 – Slideworld

Similar to Slideshare, Slideworld is another great sharing site, though it is less focused on the social aspect and more on the content creation side of things. In addition to sharing your content on this site, you can also upload templates to share. This might be an effective strategy if you're in the B2B space and you want put together a template that potential customers can use, however they do have a lot of templates that are more consumer focused.

#22 - SlideBloom

SlideBoom is different than all the other content-sharing sites in the sense that it seems to be exclusively for businesses, and it offers users the ability to convert presentations into HTML5 formats. The site also features a wide variety of groups and communities that can be joined, discussing different topics.

#23 – Scribd

Scribd recently converted into a platform similar to Kindle Unlimited, allowing users to read an unlimited number of books and audiobooks each month for a small fee of $8.99, however they still allow people to upload and monetize their content on their platform. What can you publish on Scribd? They support just about any kind of written content you can think of. Here is a list of the type of content you can publish with them:

- Creative writing
- Recipes
- How-to-guides
- Books
- Presentations
- School papers
- Spreadsheets
- Original essays
- Travel guides
- Legal documents
- Business forms
- Sheet music
- Study guides

- Academic papers
- Poetry
- Catalogs
- Speeches
- Letters
- Historical documents
- Scientific data
- Infographics
- Source documents
- Magazines
- Newspapers
- Comics
- Resumes

Create an Infographic and Share it with the World -

Infographics are a great way to connect with people who are more visually stimulated, while repurposing your content at the same time. Keep in mind that with the ever-increasing popularity of infographics the quality of most of them has dropped, so if you're designing your own, try to make it stand out from the crowd. Need an example? Check out this infographic from Entreprenuer.com. Here are a few tips that will help you stay on top of your infographic-making game:

1. Tell a story: Make sure your infographic tells a compelling story. While a visual depiction of your top ten list may be neat, it won't help you stand out from the crowd.
2. Make it "Bite-Sized": Make sure your infographic is broken into "bite-size" or small chunks that are easy to digest, and understand. Nothing will kill someone's interest faster than an infographic that is overwhelming.
3. Use Stats: If the content you're repurposing has info that can be

conveyed in a statistical way then make sure to do so-- however, don't limit yourself to pie charts and bar graphs. Get creative with it. Here's a really great infographic showing some research on different types of beliefs and their changes, displayed in a fun and captivating way.

4. Left to right: In the western world we're trained to read from left to right, in a downward motion. While this may seem pretty basic, a lot of people happen to forget it when they're designing things. Keep this in mind when you're mapping things out.

I don't know about you, but I definitely have an inner designer waiting to burst forth-- can you relate? Then you might want to leave the design work up to the professionals. You can have great infographics made on Fiverr.com, Visual.ly, and 99Designs. If you want the best bang for your buck, I would recommend trying 99 Designs first, as you will get a wide variety of options to choose from. However, if you're feeling creative and want to give it a try, or you're on a tight budget, you can use these sites to help: Infogram, Picktochart, or Canva.com.

#24 – Post Your Infographic on Slideshare

And you thought Slideshare was just for slideshows? Nope you can also post your infographics there.

#25 – Visual.ly

Visual.ly is mainly a design service company. It's similar to 99 Designs, but they've built a community around infographics and designs similar to how Hubspot has built a community around marketing automation. They have community pages where you'll be able to upload your own content. They don't accept everything, however, so you want to make sure your stuff fits their reach. Visualy.ly is also a great resource for finding good ideas of ways to communicate visually.

#26 – Scribd

As mentioned before, Scribd is a great place to upload your content to help you reach a new audience, and your infographics can also be shared there.

#27-30 - Pinterest, Google+, Tumblr, Flickr

These social networks take a clear advantage when it comes to displaying visual content. If you are creating infographics, you should give each of them serious consideration.

#31 Blogs in Your Space

Infographics should be easily shared and reposted by viewers. Reach out to the top 20-30 blogs in your space and ask them if they'd like to share your graphic on their site. It's faster than guest posting and different from what their readers might currently be doing. This can also be great way to gain exposure if you're referencing something on their blog as source material.

Create a Video -

Video content is becoming more and more common as mobile technology has improved to support it and major platforms have grown their own video solutions. Just look at your own Facebook feed. The amount of videos that show up has grown a lot over the years. YouTube doubles as a large search engine, and Google ranks good YouTube videos in its search results. It's safe to say that turning some of your content into quality videos is definitely worth the time and money.

That being said, you don't need to invest thousands of dollars in fancy video equipment and pay hundreds of dollars to have your videos edited. Surprisingly, there are a lot of great tools available right at your fingertips. These days, smart phone cameras come in pretty high quality, and they have built in microphones, however, if you don't enjoy selfie-point-of-view videos, you can invest in something a little better. I use a basic Canon DSLR to film all of my videos. My one pro tip? If you choose a DSLR to film, be sure to invest in a good microphone that attaches to the camera, or a lavaliere mic that attaches to your body.

Do you feel a bit too "camera shy" to make your own videos? You just may be in luck depending on what your videos are about. Rather than being front and center in the screen, you can use software such as Screen Flow (for Macs), or Camtasia (for PCs) to capture your computer screen activity. This is really helpful when it comes to making how-to guides, and it is super cost effective. That's it on videos for now-- I don't want to go very far into best practices because that is a whole other course on its own, and I believe there are people out there who can do a lot better job of teaching about them than I can.

#36 – YouTube

It's safe to assume that YouTube is the biggest and most popular video-sharing site on the internet. It is a great platform for almost any type of content, and it is pretty easy for users to set up and build their own channels.

#37 - Vimeo

Vimeo is similar to YouTube, but it definitely has more of an "artistic feel" to it. The content that is uploaded and shared there is less user-generated, and more filmmaker inspired. This is the ideal platform if you're content has a real professional polish, and is a little more than just your standard "talking head" YouTube video. Vimeo also offers some great paid hosting options if you choose to embed your videos on a private area of your website.

#38 – Viddler

Unlike YouTube and Vimeo, Viddler is a B2B platform that you can use to create and host interactive videos. It's much less a distribution platform (like YouTube) and more of a software product. This is a great option if you are looking to add some polish and interactivity that you probably won't get from YouTube.

#39 –Facebook

Facebook has really been growing its video platform, and there is a lot of talk about it favoring video content in its stream algorithms. This is perfect for anyone who wants to make some short, interesting videos and upload them directly to their Facebook page, rather than putting them on YouTube, and then sharing them on your page. You might even get some extra love from Facebook and its extended audience if you do.

#40 –Likes.com

Likes.com is a newer social networking site that is quickly becoming popular with teenagers around the world. It has just released a new feature in its app that allows users to live stream an event from their cellphone. If you are planning on doing an event, or you would like to stream something from our business, this is an awesome tool that is completely free, and will help you build up your audience. Full disclosure as I write this-- I happen to be an employee of MyLikes, who owns Likes.com. However, the feature is still pretty neat, and has huge potential to change the way that content is created. Imagine being at a protest, and being able to live stream it to your audience. This would also work at a big sporting event, such as a football game. Likes.com allows you to share your experience with your audience, instantly. The possibilities are endless.

Create a Podcast -

Podcasts have ebbed and flowed in popularity, but due to the recent improvements in cell phones and cellular technology they have made an incredible comeback. They have helped to breathe new life into brands such as *NPR*, and *This American Life*, as podcasts allow them to reach a younger, more urban audience that doesn't really listen to the radio very often. In fact, *This American Life's* newest podcast "Serial" has over 1 million downloads per episode! Even major brands like the "Spartan Race," and *New York Time's* best-selling author, Tim Ferris, have started to create podcasts of their own. They are a great format for communicating a brand's story, interviewing industry experts, and explaining things to a wide audience. I am no expert in creating podcasts, so I am going to direct you to two courses that will help you find podcast-success of your own.

The First Course is *the Podcast Blue Print* by Andrew Ferebee, creator of the *Knowledge for Men* Podcast. It is an interesting Podcast that explores issues of masculinity in modern society. It's great for men and women who are in gender-issue related fields, and even entrepreneurship.

You can access Andrews course on Udemy, at the link below.
https://www.udemy.com/the-podcast-blueprint/?dtcode=vaD8AXp258mH

The second course I would recommend is called *Podcasters Paradise* and is run by John Lee Dumas of *Entrepreneur on Fire*. John runs two successful podcasts, and a variety of side businesses. His podcasts usually feature interesting authors, entrepreneurs, and small business owners. His course however is about six times the cost of Andrews. It may be more expensive, but you definitely can't argue with success.
Here is the link to his course.
http://www.entrepreneuronfire.com/podcastersparadise

Does the idea of committing to another long-term distribution and content creation channel seem overwhelming to you? I am right there with you, however, there are some ways to do podcasts without having to create a weekly or monthly episode. You can always create an audio course, or a short five to six episode podcast that people can download and take in at their own leisure. You might never reach a number-one rank with this strategy, but at least you can provide some great content for your audience without a binding time commitment.

Turn your Content into an Informative Webinar

Webinars, like podcasts, have exploded with popularity due to improvements in video streaming and internet speeds. Webinars are a great way to convert site visitors into paying customers. Webinars allow your audience to interact with you in real-time, in a way that other formats don't allow. From a consumer standpoint it's like getting access to a coach or expert for a short period of time. This type of interaction will result in a boost of brand trust and conversion rates, when done correctly.

Not sure how to go about the content creation aspect of this idea? There are a lot of tools available to help you create and distribute your webinar. There's also a pretty neat course created by Lewis Howes of *School of Greatness,* a podcast that is said to be making over 1 million dollars a year, just from webinars alone. I am currently taking this course, but haven't decided to pull the trigger on my own webinar yet, at the time of this writing. If you have already converted one of your articles into a slide deck on Slideshare, most of your work is already done.

Beyond presenting and selling your content, webinars are a great way to help your customers get more from your product or service. You can offer your audience weekly advanced tips and tricks that will help customers who are more "hands-on" learners.

#40 - GoToWebinar

GoToWebinar is the gold standard in webinar technology. It's well made, and super reliable. For someone just starting out, the price can be disheartening, but it's a must if you have a more established business or brand. Maybe you are already familiar with GoToWebinar's counterpart, GoToMeeting, which is used by sales professionals around the world.

#41 - Google+ Hangouts

Google+ Hangouts is a tool from Google that allows you to do video hangouts over the internet. So why does this new video-chatting platform come in handy with repurposing your content? You can record your hangouts and post them automatically to YouTube. While this tool is free and supports many different participants, it is full of usability issues that make it less-than-ideal for people who really want to create videos with a more professional-looking polish to them. If you are, however, just looking for a low-cost (free) webinar tool that will allow for greater group collaboration, this is your best bet.

#42 WebEx by Cisco

This is another software tool used by professional sales teams around the world. While meant for a more corporate meeting environment, Webex is a good option for people who plan on hosting smaller webinars (100 people or less). It costs between 25-89 dollars a month depending on the options you choose.

#43 AnyMeeting

AnyMeeting is a new player in the webinar space, but it seems to have a lot of built-in features that are ideal for small business owners who do not have large

teams to support their content marketing efforts. It has customizable registration pages and built-in social promotion, which directly posts on your Facebook and twitter feeds, reminding people to sign up. It also has a ticketing system that allows you to sell tickets to your webinar, if that's something you want to do. It can support up to 200 participants and costs about 78 dollars per month.

QUICK TIP: If this is something you're seriously considering implementing as part of your content strategy, but you're tight on funds or scared of making a financial commitment, most of the above software allow 14-30 day free trials. So if you set up your presentation and do all the heavy lifting before you start promoting you could potentially get 1-2 webinars completed with each software, for free, without having to spend a dime.

Convert your Blog into a Snazzy E-Book -

E-books and "cheat sheets" are by far the most popular way to repurpose content. I don't think there is a single website that I visit that hasn't offered a free download or low-cost e-book at some point, however a lot of it is garbage. Keep in mind that there is a right way to do this, and a wrong way.

Many bloggers and content creators simply copy and paste their blog articles together in a semi-coherent document, and put it behind a download wall. This is a common strategy used by bloggers to help build a mailing list. It's sometimes called a content upgrade, where you offer your content in a downloadable format with additional information not found in the original article. It's a strategy I'm using in the release of this book. I've released part one as a downloadable guide to help you generate content and blog ideas, and next I will be releasing this content repurposing guide as part two.

After I will release a content strategy guide as a downloadable, and then put all the documents together with some additional information that ties it together so I can really begin to offer it as the "Ultimate Guide" to content marketing. Once the complete package is finished I will release it on Amazon.

Before we get to that though, I'll go over some basics for creating a downloadable e-book. If you want to separate yourself from the pack you need to put something together that is quality.

However if this is your first attempt at e-book publishing, you might want to set a goal of simply releasing something (anything), and then working on improving your quality with each additional release.

Self-publishing an e-book on Amazon specifically has a lot of benefits and strategies to it. Because Amazon is the largest online market place for books, and operates as a pseudo-search engine, there are strategies you can use to help your book perform in its category. This makes it easier for you to become a number one author in underwater photography, caveman cooking, or really, whatever topic you feel like talking about.

#43 - Papyrus

For a lot of people the hardest part of putting together an e-book is just that, putting it together. This is where Papyrus Editor comes in, (not to be confused with the card store in shopping malls). Instead of copying and pasting your blog content into Microsoft Word or some other text editor that does a lot of the work for you, Papyrus will use an RSS feed to pull in your content and format it into a book. First you pick out a theme from their extensive collection, then you import the content directly from your site, and all of the formatting work is automatically done for you. When you are finished with this process, Papyrus will even publish the book in the formats of your choosing, and help you sell them on your own site using "Gumroad" as a payment processor. It really is an "all-inclusive" publishing tool.

#44 – PressBooks

PressBooks is a Wordpress-based tool that is available to you for free. The good thing is, is you are accustomed to the Wordpress interface, PressBooks will seem pretty straight forward, and easy-to-use. Once you're finished, Pressbooks, just like all other tools out there, will convert it into PDF, EPUB, and MOBI formats. You can then use these formats to have your book printed via Amazon's CreateSpace. CreateSpace is free to use, however it will watermark your e-book with its own watermark, which you have to pay to remove.

#45 - Liber.io

Liber.io converts your documents from Google Drive, Dropbox, OneDrive and even Github (for you engineers out there), into an e-publishing format with a beautifully designed interface. Once you've imported your document you can start formatting it, setting up your table of contents chapters, pages, etc. They also have a variety of pre-designed templates that you can use. Once you're book is finished it will be ready for Amazon, Google Play, and iBooks on iTunes.

Places to Distribute your E-book:

#46 - Amazon Store

As mentioned before Amazon is the largest online marketplace, so not listing your book there would be pretty silly. With that being said-- there are still some things you'll want to consider. If you're not using one of the above-mentioned tools to format your book or you're doing it yourself, you might want to have someone on Odesk or Elance do it for you so that it looks professional. Often self-published books will have janky-looking formats that will almost always turn a reader off before they really get into the "meat" of your book.

The good news is: Kindle Direct Publishing (KDP) on Amazon will have your book up for sell in less than 48 hours. Authors also earn 70% of whatever the book sells in the United States, Canada, United Kingdom, Germany, India, France, Italy, Spain, Japan, Brazil, Mexico, and Australia. If you choose to enroll in

"KDP Select," your book will be available in Kindle Unlimited, which pays publishers out of the subscription pool of money. As of December 2014, that pool for the month was worth over 3 million dollars. That number should be increasing steadily over the next few years. With KDP, you also get access to a couple of promotional tools, and a countdown tool that sells your book at a discounted price for a limited time (which might be helpful to you if you are releasing a new book, but already have a back catalogue).

In addition to this, you can give your book away for free for a limited time, which will ideally help you reach the number one position in your category much faster. The only real "downfall" of using KDP is this: the digital format of your book must be exclusive to Amazon buyers. You can still print physical copies of your book elsewhere though.

#47 - iBooks

iBooks is Apple's e-book store within the iTunes marketplace. The format used by Apple allows you to build e-books that incorporate Audio and Video. However unlike Kindle publishing, iBooks are only accessible from Apple Products, so you will limit your potential audience. The good thing is, you can still publish on places like amazon, or direct to Google play.

#48- Books on Google Play

Google, like Apple, has built out its Play marketplace to sell everything digital under the sun. I wouldn't be surprised if they started integrating their Helpouts into Play in the near future, however, they don't seem to be dedicating a lot of resources to their book-publishing platform. Despite their lack of efforts to help publishers, listing your books on Google Play might help you rank higher in search results for your topic. For example, if you're an expert in big mouth bass fishing and have published a book about the subject, it might turn up in search results more frequently if it is listed on Google Play.

Turn your Content into a REAL Book -

Now that you have created your e-book, it's time to have it converted into a real book. Advances in printing technology, along with a push by Amazon, has made self-publishing easy and relatively low-cost. There are other benefits to having your book printed like bragging to your friends, or sending to potential clients. While thousands of people might publish an e-book, very few of them are going to take that extra step and get the book physically published.

#48 - Amazon CreateSpace

CreateSpace was purchased by Amazon a while back to make its self-publishing platform even more robust and seamless. If you're already publishing with Amazon, the process is pretty simple and requires only a little more formatting to make sure your book hits it's desired dimensions. You can even bulk order physical copies of your book at a low cost, if you plan on mailing a lot of copies to your friends, family, clients, etc. If you can afford it, though, you might want to eat the cost and have a few close friends buy the books at retail from Amazon and send them out. This will help your book rank higher and faster.

#49 – LuLu

LuLu has been a leader in the self-publishing, self-printing space since 2002. They offer tools and resources to help you print and market your books. You can get an estimate of how much it would cost to print your book, here. This seems like a better fit if you need to bulk order some printed books and don't want to eat the additional costs from amazon. If you're looking for more information on becoming a best-selling author on Amazon, there's a great course on Udemy by author and host of the "Side Hustle Nation," Nick Loper. I've been going through the course and it has a lot of practical tips. You can find the course here.

Turn your Content into an E-mail Course-

An email course is not going to be a good option for every content marketer, but if you operate in a space where there's a lot of free information and competition, it can definitely be a great way to get customers into your sales funnel. It can also significantly help you build trust with your brand. When done right, it is a powerful way to connect with your customers without having to do a lot of additional work. You'll want to write out your 5-10 chain emails in advance and then have some customizable fields so you can insert the customer's information. You could even get really advanced and have the customers submit homework, and have the course adjust based upon their results. But that's on another whole level, and not really practical for people with limited resources and time. But you definitely want to build in some call-to-action, or prompt of some sort that will help you find customers with buying temperatures that are rising.

#50 – Campaign Monitor

Campaign Monitor is an affordable option for those just starting out and has a variety of pricing options starting at nine dollars a month, good for smaller companies.

#51 – MailChimp

MailChimp is a favorite email provider for smaller B2C companies. I wouldn't recommend it if you have a large list or plan on growing a large list, however, Mailchimp is by far the easiest tool to use if you are just getting started, and they have a ton of resources designed to help you become a better email marketer.

#52 – Aweber

Aweber is a favorite of bloggers and B2B companies. It has some more advanced options and integrations than Mailchimp, and it is generally not very expensive. I use it because it's low-cost and it doesn't brand my emails with their stuff. In fact, I found it because I was getting some emails from bloggers using their service and saw the name in the redirect URLs.

#53 – InfusionSoft

Infusionsoft is the most powerful of all these services and also the most expensive. This might be a better option if you already have a large business and are looking to take your email marketing to the next level. It integrates with a lot of CRMs and can help you track more effectively a customer's progression through your course and sales funnel.

Conclusion -

After reading this list I know what you might be thinking, "Holy shit, there's way too many options. How am I supposed to chose which will work best for me?" That's where this section comes in, as a guide on how to better implement your content repurposing efforts. Clearly not everything listed here is appropriate for each and every content producer, nor is it exhaustive. What you chose will depend on your intention for creating content, be it education, entertainment, business, etc.

Here are the steps I would recommend if you are producing content specifically for your business:

1. Start by creating a customer profile. This means describing whom your ultimate customer is, where they are, and what types of content they typically consume. If you are already in business you most likely already have customers, and you're in luck because you can pick up the phone, give them a call, and ask them. You can also take a look at

your blog, website, and YouTube channel (or where ever you publish your content), and draw insights from those platforms. You should be able to see what type of content gets shared most often, and which articles and videos have earned you the highest amount of engagement. From there, you should be able to figure out what type of content will be most beneficial for you to repurpose, as well as what you should turn it into.

2. Choose four to five of the resources on this list where you will be distributing your content, and do a Google search to find out best practices, or a how-to guide for using them in your content strategy. You should be able to find a lot of useful resources on Google, similar to my write-up about StumbleUpon's paid discovery program. Note: I will be releasing more how-to guides and write-ups in the future-- stay tuned!

3. Spend two to three months implementing the strategies you have planned. After that time period, sit down and analyze the results. Did you get more leads? Did those leads convert, or were they less-than-ideal? Whatever your content marketing goals are, measure whether the "needle is moving in the right direction." If your plan has been working, tighten up your strategy and continue in the same direction. If not, scratch the original plan and start with something new. something new.

4. Keep in mind: even if this takes you several attempts to figure out, your company and your customers will eventually reap the rewards. Having widely-spread content on the web will increase the benefits of your SEO efforts, as well as improve your discover-ability overall, however, that doesn't mean do EVERYTHING listed in this e-book, as you want to focus your energy on what is going to give you the greatest return on your investment.

If you're a blogger, solo entrepreneur, or internet marketer, look at the formats that are most popular with a wide variety of people even if you have a very specific niche that your create content around. The reason being is that you want your content to reach as many people as possible where a business will want to reach the right type of people. Once your content is up on places like YouTube, Pinterest, Facebook, Etc. you can use the tools that those platforms provide to reach your end goal. Whether that is sales of your digital products, more subscribers to your newsletter, or just increased visibility for the sake of speaking gigs or networking. This is the same if you're an entertainment content creator as well, however you might want to focus on efforts that will drive traffic and awareness to your brand.

If you enjoyed this book or if you think it's missing anything shoot me an e-mail at Jeremiahboehner@gmail.com, or a tweet @sfboehner, or you can find me at jeremiahboehner.com

Be Sure to Check Out My Other works!